# SHAKEN
## BIBLE STUDY

TIM TEBOW

# SHAKEN
## BIBLE STUDY

DISCOVERING YOUR TRUE IDENTITY
IN THE MIDST OF LIFE'S STORMS

WITH A.J. GREGORY

WATERBROOK

Shaken Bible Study

All Scripture quotations are taken from the New American Standard Bible®. Copyright © 1960, 1962, 1963, 1968, 1971, 1972, 1973, 1975, 1977, 1995 by the Lockman Foundation. Used by permission. (www.Lockman.org).

Details in some anecdotes and stories have been changed to protect the identities of the persons involved.

Trade Paperback ISBN 978-0-7352-8989-5
eBook ISBN 978-0-7352-8990-1



Cover design by Kristopher K. Orr; cover photograph by Bryan Soderlind



Published in the United States by WaterBrook, an imprint of the Crown Publishing Group, a division of Penguin Random House LLC, New York.

WaterBrook® and its deer colophon are registered trademarks of Penguin Random House LLC.

Library of Congress Cataloging-in-Publication Data
Names: Tebow, Tim, 1987– author. | Tebow, Tim, 1987– author. Shaken.
Title: Shaken Bible study : discovering your true identity in the midst of life's storms / by Tim Tebow, with A.J. Gregory.
Description: First Edition. | Colorado Springs, Colorado : WaterBrook, 2016.
Identifiers: LCCN 2016040282 (print) | LCCN 2016044410 (ebook) | ISBN 9780735289895 (pbk.) | ISBN 9780735289901 (electronic)
Subjects: LCSH: Identity (Psychology)—Religious aspects—Christianity—Textbooks. | Success—Religious aspects—Christianity—Textbooks.
Classification: LCC BV4509.5 .T433 2016 (print) | LCC BV4509.5 (ebook) | DDC 155.2—dc23
LC record available at https://lccn.loc.gov/2016040282

Printed in the United States of America
2018

10

# Contents

# A Note from Tim

Thanks to social media, we can tell the world—in a certain number of characters or with a photograph we've taken several times and Photoshopped to death—who we are. This is me, we say, as we smile, the sun shining bright in the background, and all is well in the world. Funny how we save the best and brightest posts for Facebook or Instagram.

I wonder, though, how many people know the real us? What we look like in the morning. Or the huge fight we just had with our spouse before we stormed out of the house. Or how much we hurt because we just lost something precious.

We have this human tendency to want to project our best selves, this image of perfection, to others. I get it. I really do. But God knows who we are. He sees our hearts. He sees the deepest parts of us. After all, He knew us before we were even in our mothers' wombs. But how many of us know who we are, and how many live with that truth as their foundation?

Knowing who we are in Christ takes the guesswork out of figuring it out on our own. When we are secure in the truth, we don't have to depend on things like wins, accomplishments, beauty, money, or even our failures to define who we are. Our identity depends on God. It is based in Him because we were created by Love, in love, and for love.

Living from this truth is critical when bad times come. What do we hold on to when our world gets shaken? When the deal goes sour? When the diagnosis doesn't look good? When the future is unknown? But when we live from a place of depth, knowing whose we are, we can tackle all the emotions, like the fear, doubt, confusion, and anger that accompany trials. And more than that, we can use our stories, our skills, our talents, even those things that we think are imperfections to impact one person or many for Jesus.

I want to invite you on an adventure to live a life of purpose, passion, and meaning based on who you are in Jesus Christ. As you work through this study guide, my hope is that you will

- discover that your identity is found in Christ alone and that that foundation cannot be shaken,
- learn to endure hard times knowing that God has a plan for you,
- be challenged to live in line with your deepest, most heartfelt beliefs,
- understand the power of serving and connecting with others in meaningful ways, and
- engage in self-discovery as you figure out what matters most in light of eternity.

I admit I don't know all the answers. The faith journey is a perpetual wheel in motion where we grow, learn, and are stretched day after day. But my hope for you is that this Bible study will deepen your relationship with God and help you reach others in ways that leave a lasting imprint.

# How to Use This Guide

Whether you're a new Christian or a seasoned one, whether you work through this book with a small group or on your own, this study guide is designed to help you deepen your faith, learn about yourself (and others), and be encouraged to live a life that matters.

The study is divided into four sessions, and each session opens with a big idea; offers a set of in-depth discussion questions drawn from the DVD teaching, the Bible, and my book *Shaken;* and closes with prayer. The "Individual Reflection, Study, and Action" portion is meant for you to study on your own if you are using this guide in a group setting. This is your opportunity to meditate on what you've learned and apply it to your life in a practical way. Finally, I share a prayer from me to God on your behalf. As I was working on this study guide, I thought about you. I prayed for you. And I believe God will show you just how much He loves you and will remind you that He's got an awesome plan for your life. This is true, even if what you're going through looks a lot different than what you had planned or expected.

What do you need before you dive in? Though the Scripture portions to be discussed are included in this guide (New American Standard Bible version), you might want to have a Bible or a Bible app handy so you can look them up in the translation of your choice. And while space is provided for you to jot down notes, consider using a journal or digital device for additional writing. While you can certainly work through this guide without reading my book, you'll maximize your experience if you do.

If you're reading *Shaken* for the first time, follow the schedule below to coordinate with this study guide:

- Before session 1, read *Shaken* chapters 1 and 2.
- Before session 2, read chapters 3, 4, and 5.
- Before session 3, read chapters 6 and 7.
- Before session 4, read chapters 8, 9, and 10.

I'm excited to see what God is going to do in your life!

"It's tempting to define ourselves or to measure our worth by the external—by how much money we have, by how we look, by the applause of others. The list is long. Think about this. Who are you when everything is going great—when the money is in the bank, when your home life is peaceful, when your future seems certain? And who are you when your world is shaken—when your bank account is overdrawn, when your relationship is on the fritz, when you haven't a clue what tomorrow holds? Sometimes it takes a challenging time to really find out."

—from *Shaken*

SESSION

# WHO ARE YOU?

## **BIG IDEA** for This Session

We should never let others, material stuff, or circumstances tell us who we are; we should always be defined by our identity in Jesus Christ.

The world does not define you, but it certainly does try to. And often, we let it.

One day we fall into the trap of believing who we are has everything to do with our job, our impressive résumé, our good-looking spouse, the amount of money we have in our bank account, the framed degrees on our wall, or a championship run. And the next, the world mercilessly drags away and destroys everything it once made us believe defined our identity. We get fired and struggle for months to find another job. We experience a failure that overshadows our past triumphs or accolades. We file for bankruptcy. We lose the game. We lose the house. We lose a loved one.

And when our world is shaken to such a degree, we're left wondering, *Who am I?*

This is more than just a philosophical question. Know this: *the world doesn't get to define us, because God already did.* We were created by Love, in love, and for love. If we know Jesus, we are His children. Knowing who we are in Christ and being rooted in that identity breathes life into us. It energizes us. It changes us. It gives us purpose. It gives us meaning. It makes us able to handle whatever doubt, crisis, or negativity comes our way. When we stop striving to let the world, our friends, our neighbors, or society define who we are and instead start living as children of the King of kings, we can live at our best.

Because our identity is secure, we don't have to ride the roller coaster of life. We don't have to live up in the highs or down in the lows. No matter what happens, we can live with confidence knowing we stand on a sure foundation.

## GETTING STARTED

In what ways or by what measures have you defined your identity over the years?

## SESSION 1 VIDEO: WHO ARE YOU?

In this video segment I talk about the source of our identity, Jesus Christ. When we know whose we are, we understand that we each have purpose and we each matter. When we give God whatever we have to offer, amazing things can happen!

*Watch Video Session 1. While viewing the video, use the spaces below to record key ideas or any thoughts you want to remember.*

### Video Teaching Notes

It's not about who you are; it's about whose you are.

We are God's poem, created with a purpose.

The multitude is fed with five loaves and two fish—with twelve baskets of leftovers!

Jesus is not *just* enough; He is always *more* than enough.

God used a Scripture reference painted on eye black to do something amazing. God wants to perform miracles in you and through you too.

## Video Discussion

1. Have you ever allowed the world to define you? If so, what made you fall for it?

2. How does the knowledge that God has a plan for you (see Ephesians 2:10) help you endure hard times?

3. In this video I share how God used the Bible verse references on my eye black to influence others. Can you think of a situation in your life that God used in a surprising way to influence another person or even many people?

## TALK ABOUT IT

1. Here are some common ways that people define their identity:

    - a family role like mother, father, husband, wife, son, daughter
    - a job or career like coach, teacher, entrepreneur, student, business owner, consultant
    - a talent or skill like athlete, musician, writer, graphic designer, actor, artist

    You may define yourself in one or several ways. But out of all the possibilities, what would you say are one or two of the more important ways you define your identity?

2. Here's a verse from the Bible that tells how we were made "in the image of God":

> Then God said, "Let Us make man in Our image, according to Our likeness; and let them rule over the fish of the sea and over the birds of the sky and over the cattle and over all the earth, and over every creeping thing that creeps on the earth." God created man in His own image, in the image of God He created him; male and female He created them. (Genesis 1:26–27)

What does this mean to you as it concerns living in the "real world"?

3. Think about the times you have disliked something about yourself or doubted your abilities. Do you think that in those times you were, in a way, telling God that He didn't know what He was doing when He made you in His image? Why or why not?

4. Here's another amazing Bible passage:

   For You formed my inward parts;
   You wove me in my mother's womb.
   I will give thanks to You, for I am fearfully and
   wonderfully made;
   Wonderful are Your works,
   And my soul knows it very well.
   (Psalm 139:13–14)

   What factors in your life make it easier to believe that you are "fearfully and wonderfully made"? What makes it difficult to believe that phrase?

5. What would your confidence level be if you believed wholeheartedly that you are made in His image?

6. Mark Stuart, the former lead singer for the group Audio Adrenaline, lost his singing voice and had to give up his music career at the height of his success (see his story on pages 31–35 in *Shaken*). You too may have experienced a significant loss that defined a part of your identity, perhaps a lifelong dream of owning your own business, being accepted into a certain college, or creating the "perfect" family. How did the loss make you feel initially?

7. Mark says that despite his disappointment, he chose to believe that "God was authoring a bigger picture" (page 33). Reflect on your answer to the previous question: What evidence of God at work can you now see in your own experience of loss?

8. *Purpose* is one of those words that people have tossed around so much that it's hard to know exactly what it means. I believe that it's intertwined with your identity in Jesus Christ. My purpose never was playing football. Instead, football was a platform, a means through which I could love Jesus and love others. What platform(s) do you see that God has given you to represent Him?

9. When Jesus decided to feed the multitude, all he needed was a boy's five loaves and two fish. That small meal was more than enough. How does this encourage you to give Jesus whatever it is you have to offer?

10. Describe a time when God was at work in your life and you didn't even realize it.

## WRAP UP

Today we have learned how important our identity in Christ is in accomplishing the purpose God has for our lives. Let's close our time together in prayer. Here are some ideas from this session that can guide our conversation with God:

- Thank God for your being created in His image, for His divine thumbprint on your life.
- Ask the Holy Spirit to remind you in times of doubt or confusion of your identity in Christ and the plan and purpose He has for you.
- Ask God to open your eyes to how you can live in a new way and change your heart, not trusting what the world says but what He says.
- Pray for God to reveal opportunities where He can use you to change the life of one person or the lives of many.

## INDIVIDUAL REFLECTION, STUDY, AND ACTION

When you know whose you are, it changes everything. It changes how you live, how you interact with others, how you connect with God, how you view and grow in circumstances that make you feel shaken. When you believe with all your heart that you are the object of God's love, it can change your actions.

1. Think about an area in your life where you struggle with this belief about how God loves you. How does it affect the way you live, what you think about, and how you act?

2. When your identity is grounded in whose you are, it doesn't mean you'll never feel the weight of emotions like self-doubt or disappointment. When you feel yourself getting sidetracked, cling to God.

   Picture a child who wakes up from a nightmare,

tears falling down his cheeks like a waterfall, his tiny body shaking from fear. Picture his mother rushing to his bedside to scoop the child up and console him in her loving arms. Picture the child wrapping his arms around her, nestling his head into the crook of her neck. As the tears continue to fall, he holds on for dear life, never wanting to let go, trusting in her soft words of comfort that everything is okay. This is what it means to cling.

There are many instances in the Bible where we are encouraged to "cling," or hold fast, to God (see Deuteronomy 10:20; 13:4; Joshua 23:8; 2 Kings 18:6; Psalm 63:8; 119:31; Jeremiah 13:11). One way you can cling to God is by knowing and believing what He says in His Word about you. You might want to memorize these verses so that in a pressure moment you won't forget who you *really* are:

> For we are His workmanship, created in Christ
> Jesus for good works, which God prepared
> beforehand so that we would walk in them.
> (Ephesians 2:10)

> For You formed my inward parts;
> You wove me in my mother's womb.

I will give thanks to You, for I am fearfully and
wonderfully made;
Wonderful are Your works,
And my soul knows it very well. (Psalm
139:13–14)

Tell yourself over and over:

- "I am created for a reason."
- "I am created in the image of God."
- "God's got a good plan for me."

When you are rooted in what He says, you can live confidently because you know these things:

- He loves you, no matter what.
- He has a purpose for you, no matter what.
- He can use you, no matter what.

Knowing and living these truths will change your life.

## MY PRAYER FOR YOU

*Dear Jesus, I thank You for the person reading this book right now. Please reveal to them how special and important they are. Remind them that they are created on purpose by Love, in love, and for love. If they're in the midst of a personal storm, I pray that You will tell them in their hearts that You have an amazing plan in store, no matter what they are going through. Give them strength and wisdom to trust Your purpose for their life. Make them more aware of the platform You have given them, and help them to walk through each day with confidence because they belong to You. In Your name, amen.*

## PREPARE FOR THE NEXT SESSION

Before the group meets again, read chapters 3, 4, and 5 in *Shaken*.

"When who you are is grounded in whose you are, you realize it doesn't matter what life throws your way. When your world starts to shake or fall apart, you can lean into Him for security, for safety. You can get through even the toughest of circumstances because God is on your side. He loves you more than you know. And He's got everything under control more than you know. He's got plans for you. Awesome plans! You and God are unstoppable!"

—from *Shaken*

SESSION

# WHEN STORMS COME

## BIG IDEA for This Session

The more you make the choice to live above your feelings and trust God, the stronger your faith becomes.

Many of us have endured a time of crisis. A persistent addiction. An unanswered prayer. A loss of a job. A difficult or severed relationship. In John 16:33 Jesus told us that life wouldn't be easy. In fact, He promised that we would have tribulation. Some translations use the terms "trouble," "trials," or "sorrows." Whatever you want to call it, it boils down to hard times.

But that's not the end of the story. Here's the good news: Jesus also promised us peace even in the midst of these things. It's pretty amazing when you think about it. Is it possible to have peace when you don't know when your next paycheck is coming? Or when the doctors aren't sure how to make you well? Or when the dream you've worked so hard to accomplish runs aground? Jesus says, "Yes. It is possible."

Getting cut from three NFL teams and being told over and over that I'm not good enough to play quarterback wasn't easy. There were times I doubted God's plan for my life, asking Him, "Where are You? I thought You had this." There were times I couldn't help but hear the negative voices in the media bashing me every which way. In these moments, I had to go back to what God said about me.

I had to remind myself that He has a plan. That He has a purpose. And I had to choose to trust God over and over and over again.

Doubts will come. Negative voices, whether from others or ourselves, will come. So what do you do when you face these things? Trust God. Choose faith. I've learned that when we choose faith over fears, over overwhelming emotions, over negativity, over disappointments, and over pain, we will overcome. Why? Because Jesus did. And He tells us that through Him, we can too.

## GETTING STARTED

A big trend in the early 2000s was wearing T-shirts from the popular clothing line No Fear. They featured inspirational slogans such as "Don't pursue your dreams, chase 'em down and tackle 'em" and "Fear has killed more men than time." While living without fear definitely takes more effort than throwing on a quote-filled tee, what would your life look like if you had no fear?

## SESSION 2 VIDEO: WHEN STORMS COME

In this video segment, I talk about a well-known biblical underdog named David who, by trusting God, beat the odds and defeated a giant. But life isn't only full of magnificent battles that end with victory. We go through some lows too. It's important to trust God in both times.

*Watch Video Session 2. While viewing the video, use the spaces below to record key ideas or any thoughts you want to remember.*

### Video Teaching Notes

David trusted that his God was bigger than any giant who was ever going to get in his way.

We serve the same God who helped David defeat Goliath.

Jesus told us that tough times would come, but in the meantime we have to take heart, or courage (John 16:33).

We need to choose courage, to have and keep the faith, every day.

If you trust God with and offer Him everything, even your bitterness and pain, He will not waste it.

## Video Discussion

1. David trusted God and faced the challenge to battle against Goliath, even though he was young and inexperienced, even when everyone around him thought he was nuts. How does David's bold trust inspire you to face your giants?

2. Despite her battle with cancer, Chelsie chose courage and faith time and time again. Describe a time you made a choice to trust God even though your circumstances looked bleak.

3. Do you struggle with bitterness? Maybe you're holding on to the pain of a heartbreak. Why is it hard for you to consider surrendering that pain or bitterness to God?

## TALK ABOUT IT

1. In John 16:33 Jesus says, "These things I have spoken to you, so that in Me you may have peace. In the world you have tribulation, but take courage; I have overcome the world." Jesus reminds us that He has overcome the world, that we have a choice between peace or turmoil. Have you ever experienced peace in the midst of a storm?

2. How does this verse encourage you when you're fighting through disappointment or fear?

3. Read Psalm 16:8:

> I have set the LORD continually before me;
> Because He is at my right hand, I will not be
> shaken.

What is the promise that God offers us in this verse?

4. What condition must be met for the promise to be true?

5. Something pretty awesome happens when we continually set the Lord before us: we build up "muscle memory." We strengthen our faith. We grow in maturity. When we exercise our faith muscle in this way, it grows. In what ways can you set the Lord continually before you?

6. On the night before He was to be crucified, Jesus wrestled with God, His Father, while praying in the Garden of Gethsemane: "Father, if You are willing, remove this cup from Me" (Luke 22:42). Jesus's heart was torn between doing what He knew was necessary and being aware of what it required. Ultimately, He obeyed His Father's will and modeled willingness and obedience in the face of fear. Can you recall a time in your life when you felt God telling you to do something but you were afraid to do it?

7. Reflect back on your previous answer. Were you obedient despite your conflicting desires? Why or why not?

8. Just as Jesus chose love over fear, in what ways can you let love dominate over fear?

9. If you struggle with pain or bitterness from a situation that broke your heart, are you willing, today, to take a step of faith and offer it to God with an open hand?

10. How can a tough time you have been through inspire or encourage someone else?

## WRAP UP

Today we have learned that God is always fighting for us and that no matter what we are going through, we can have peace if we choose to keep trusting Him. Let's close our time together in prayer. Here are some ideas from this session that can guide our conversation with God:

- Thank God for His unfailing love and for being the object of His love. Ask Him to help you show that love to others.
- Pray that God gives you a spirit of courage and strengthens your faith so you can shine His light to those around you.
- Surrender your fears, your worries, and your concerns to God, and ask Him to fill you with His redeeming hope, which is more powerful than any storm.
- Praise God in advance for His faithfulness and provision in your circumstances and that no matter what it looks like, you believe in your heart that He's got this.

## INDIVIDUAL REFLECTION, STUDY, AND ACTION

1. Reflect on the apostle Paul's encouragement to "pray without ceasing" (1 Thessalonians 5:17) and to "be anxious for nothing, but in everything by prayer and supplication with thanksgiving let your requests be made known to God. And the peace of God, which surpasses all comprehension, will guard your hearts and your minds in Christ Jesus" (Philippians 4:6–7).

   When you are faced with your next problem, offer it to God through prayer. And keep doing this. Don't just pray one time. Turn to your heavenly Father whenever you feel anxious about your relationship, uncertain about your job, or encumbered by the weight of emotions like panic, fear, or disappointment. What challenge or problem in your life today—a giant or something smaller—do you need to offer to God in prayer? Take time right now to pray about it.

2. At some point in time, we are all going to hear someone say some not-so-nice things about us. Maybe a parent constantly told you growing up that you were good for nothing. Maybe you posted something on social media about wanting to write a book and got stung by a stranger who said that it's too hard and you'll probably never do it. Maybe your self-esteem keeps taking hits because society tells you that you're not pretty enough, smart enough, rich enough, or in good-enough shape. Maybe you struggle with self-negativity and believe there's no way you'll get the promotion or that you're unqualified to serve in a certain position at church.

   Whatever the hurtful criticism, damaging comment, or self-doubt, in these moments remember that what God says about you is what's most important. Do this by meditating on the following truths from Scripture. You might also consider posting these affirmations somewhere you can see them every day, like on your phone, computer, coffee mug, or water bottle.

| | |
|---|---|
| 2 Thessalonians 2:13 | You are chosen by God. |
| Galatians 3:26 | You are a child of God. |
| 2 Corinthians 5:17 | You are a new creation in Christ. |
| Ephesians 2:10 | You are God's masterpiece. |

| | |
|---|---|
| Romans 5:8 | You are deeply loved. |
| Ephesians 1:3 | You are blessed with spiritual blessings in heavenly places. |

## MY PRAYER FOR YOU

*Dear Jesus, thank You for how deep Your love is for the person reading these words. Your love will never fail them. I pray for the one who is struggling with fear. As Your Word says in Psalm 56:3, may they put their trust in You, and You alone. You are faithful and You will come through for them. I pray they won't allow the negative voices of others or even themselves to rule their minds. Speak into their hearts. May they live in a way that reflects what You say about them more than the Evil One, more than the naysayers, and more than their inner critic. In Your name, amen.*

## PREPARE FOR THE NEXT SESSION

Before the group meets again, read chapters 6 and 7 in *Shaken*.

“The more you make the choice to live above your feelings, to trust God instead of what you may feel like doing, the stronger your faith becomes. It’s not about being perfect. We will always be on a journey of growing closer to God. I can tell you that I’ve messed up before and I’ll mess up again. Chances are you will too. Choose faith. Choose to trust God more than what you feel. Choose to believe in Him whether or not you feel like it.”

—from *Shaken*

SESSION

# OTHERS MATTER

## **BIG IDEA** for This Session

Having people speak truth into your life helps you live at your best and strive to be better than average, more than ordinary, far above "normal."

If I say the word *church,* what's the first thing that comes to your mind? If I were to guess, I'd say a building, probably the one where you go on Sunday. But church is not a four-walled structure where people dress up and spend an hour or two once a week. The church is the body of believers. It's you and me. God designed us to be in relationship with Him first and foremost, and then with others. One of the ways that we actually live church every day is by being in relationship with people. It's about connecting with others. Inspiring them. Challenging them. And they do the same for us.

We need to have friends in our lives who are going to have our back, who are going to support us and share the truth in love. We need friends who can carry us when we're weak. We need friends we can count on. I love this verse:

> And if one can overpower him who is alone, two can resist him. A cord of three strands is not quickly torn apart. (Ecclesiastes 4:12)

This is God's reminder that we are not meant to do life alone.

You know what happens when we surround ourselves with people who inspire and challenge us in life and in our faith? We grow. We learn how to live in the uniqueness with which God created us. Instead of wanting to be like everyone else, we can make the most of what God gave us. We can have the courage to use even the things that make us stand out in the crowd in ways that can impact others. We can begin to live at our best.

## GETTING STARTED

An old Swedish proverb goes something like this: "Shared joy is a double joy; shared sorrow is half a sorrow." What do you value most in your friendships with others, and why? What would you say other people value about you?

## SESSION 3 VIDEO: OTHERS MATTER

In this video segment, I talk about being inspired by a little boy and two of his friends who refused to leave their buddy's side, no matter what. These boys weren't concerned about just being normal like everyone else. They stood out from the crowd and dared to be different.

*Watch Video Session 3. While viewing the video, use the spaces below to record key ideas or any thoughts you want to remember.*

### Video Teaching Notes

We need to fight for people that others might not find impressive and that can't fight for themselves.

We need friends who are going to stick by our side, who will share truth and grace with us.

When you try to fit in and be like everyone else, you miss the chance to do something special.

When we are willing to be a little different, to show a little courage, to show a little bonus, God can do great things in and through us.

### Video Discussion

1. Was there a particular time when friends reached out and went above and beyond to show you their love and commitment, like Sherwin's friends did for him?

2. While it can be easy to put on a facade and hide the parts of ourselves where we struggle, we can grow as individuals and deepen our faith when we are vulnerable with others who have our best interests at heart. Who sees you for exactly who you are? Who knows your weaknesses?

3. A sense of belonging is a human need. Problem is, sometimes we want so bad to be like everyone else that we never have a chance to be special, unique, the way God created us to be. Do you struggle with wanting to fit in?

## TALK ABOUT IT

1. Describe a time you did something, perhaps outside your comfort zone or in the face of resistance, to stick up for a friend.

2. Can you recall a time when someone stuck up for you in the same way?

3. Proverbs 13:20 offers some great advice: "He who walks with wise men will be wise, but the companion of fools will suffer harm." Think about the friends around you.

Which do you count on for encouragement, guidance, and support when you need it most? List some examples of what these friends have done to be "wise" in your life.

4. Here's another impactful message from Proverbs: "Iron sharpens iron, so one man sharpens another" (27:17). Spiritual and personal growth come when we are open to correction, willing to accept hard truth, and able to appreciate another's perspective when we have tunnel vision. Similarly, we must be just as willing to dish out hard truth and strengthen others in their faith when they need it. Think of a time someone in your life had to speak the truth in love. How did you react?

5. In *Shaken,* Robyn talks about being born with cerebral palsy and having to learn to walk with a walker. She says, "When I looked in the mirror, I didn't see a teenage girl, I saw what I was convinced everyone else saw: a disability" (page 126). Have you ever felt insecure or "less than" because of something that made you different or stand out from those around you?

6. What's the difference between how we see ourselves and how God sees us?

7. While most of us (hopefully) would never be rude or disrespectful to someone with a physical or mental impairment, think about a time you may have been less than kind to someone close to you or to a stranger. What can you do going forward to show God's love to others and reflect the command offered in Ephesians 4:32: "Be kind to one another, tender-hearted, forgiving each other, just as God in Christ also has forgiven you"?

8. Share about someone in your life you have been influenced by because they have used something that makes them unique (whether a disability, life experience, or character trait) to make an impact on others.

9. What can you do to thank the person you named in the previous question?

10. How can you, starting today, begin to appreciate your uniqueness and stand out for Jesus?

## WRAP UP

Today we have learned how important it is to be a good friend and to have good friends, how those relationships can lead us to living a life rooted in our uniqueness. Let's close with prayer. Here are some ideas from this session that can guide our conversation with God:

- Thank God for the people in your life who have invested or are currently investing in you through prayer, encouragement, and wisdom. Ask Him to shape you and enlarge your heart to be that kind of person to others.
- Ask God to bring people along your path to do life with, particularly if you struggle with loneliness.
- Praise God for creating people to do life with, and ask Him to give you a spirit of compassion and generosity to love those you interact with each day.
- Thank God for making you unique, special. Ask Him for opportunities in which He can use you to help others and reflect His glory, even through what you may consider a flaw or imperfection.

## INDIVIDUAL REFLECTION, STUDY, AND ACTION

1. Think about the friends that you go to for advice, wisdom, and discernment when you have tough decisions to make. Who has your ear? Are you quick to listen to the person who tells you what you want to hear? Or do you listen to the one who tells you the truth? Reflect on whether or not you may need to rethink where you get advice.

2. Take time for some personal inventory. Think about how you would feel being on the receiving end of your words. Are you a person others should listen to or ignore? Do you give sound, prayerful advice, or do you say whatever is on your mind without thinking about it first? Are there some areas in which you need to grow spiritually or otherwise? What is the first step you can take to begin to make those changes?

3. When you start to embrace and even celebrate how unique God made you, you can begin to do extraordinary things. You can begin to see yourself through His eyes. You can be motivated and inspired to go against the grain. Do you struggle with self-doubt? Not sure how God can use you? Prayerfully reflect on the uniqueness with which you were created, whether one or a combination of talents, skills, a disability, and/or life experiences.

4. List three people in your life you can impact wherever God has planted you at this time. How can you make a difference in their lives?

## MY PRAYER FOR YOU

*Dear Jesus, thank you for creating the person who is reading this book right now, making them unique, extraordinary, far above "normal." Thank You that You have made them for a purpose and that You have amazing things in store for them. I pray that You would put in place people around them to speak truth and life into their hearts. And help them to lift others up in the same way. In Your name, amen.*

## PREPARE FOR THE NEXT SESSION

Before the group meets again, read chapters 8, 9, and 10 in *Shaken*.

"It's amazing what happens when we help someone when we're feeling helpless. This doesn't have to be some big task or a save-the-world project. You don't have to raise a million dollars. You don't have to go on a mission trip next week. (Although these are all great things, and if you want to, by all means, go for it.) Think simple. In terms of those around you, send an encouraging text to a friend. Take time to listen, really listen, to another. Make some chicken soup for someone who is sick. Instead of blabbing on and on about your problems, find out what another person is going through. Pray for someone instead of always asking that person to pray for you."

—from *Shaken*

SESSION

# A LEGACY-DRIVEN LIFE

## BIG IDEA for This Session

It doesn't matter how many games we win or lose, how much money we have, or how successful we are. What matters is whether or not we are living for Jesus and leaving a mark beyond our lives.

When we know whose we are, it changes how we live. We can live with purpose. We can live knowing that even our best successes, our most favorable wins, our glory days, our most expensive and biggest toys don't matter in the big picture. What matters is the legacy we leave behind.

Who we are has to be bigger than what we do. Who we are has to be bigger than what we own, what we look like, those we know, or where we live. Who we are has to transcend the temporal. It has to carry a purpose that echoes through eternity.

What are we known for? Do we want to be defined by binging on Netflix? Or being the most fashionable? Or for always dampening a mood with our negativity? Do we want to be known for how many books we've sold, how many social-media followers we have, or how many people like us?

The most important decision we will ever make is to accept Jesus Christ as our Lord and Savior. But the abundant life Jesus came to this earth to give us encompasses more than just saying a prayer. It's about living for Him. Making a difference. Taking a stand. Doing something. We may not be able to impact a million people for Jesus, but we can certainly impact one.

God wants to use us. But we need to accept the call. We need to say yes. Whether that means encouraging a neighbor, forgiving a friend, loving on a person that you've been shying away from because they look different. It's amazing what can happen when you step out in faith and choose to live and make choices that have a lasting impact.

## GETTING STARTED

What lasts forever?

## SESSION 4 VIDEO: A LEGACY-DRIVEN LIFE

In this video segment, I talk about how we all have the ability to do something that matters. I'm not talking money, fame, or power, but making a difference in the life of one person, or many.

*Watch Video Session 4. While viewing the video, use the spaces below to record key ideas or any thoughts you want to remember.*

### Video Teaching Notes

One person can change everything.

We all have the ability to do something.

What really matters is giving what you have to make a difference in the lives of others.

Are you willing to give your time, your energy, your money, or your resources to make a difference?

My goal has always been to live a life of significance, of meaning. We do this by loving God and loving others.

## Video Discussion

1. Describe a time in your life when you were so consumed by planning or preparing for an event or a life transition

(whether the birth of a child, a move, a job change, and so on) that you lost perspective. What did someone say or do to help shift your attention away from the details so you could step back and allow God to do something powerful?

2. It's easy to lose perspective when we get caught up in our problems, our failures, the times we've fallen short, or what we want that we don't have. How can you gain a new vantage point by doing something for someone else?

3. Beauty, health, money, wins—they're all temporary. How can prioritizing things with eternal value free you from fixating on the superficial?

## TALK ABOUT IT

1. I'm a big believer in the statement "If you don't stand for something, you'll fall for anything." Talk about a stand you have taken that has impacted something or someone else.

2. What do you want to be known for?

3. In *Shaken* (pages 165–67), I talk about how I've never audibly heard from God, how I've often wrestled with making decisions in the absence of God telling me *exactly* what to do or what choice to make. In what ways do you believe you have heard God speak to your heart?

4. How do you intentionally seek to hear from God?

5. I often share about being drawn to talk to certain people. Have you ever been in a situation where you felt God in your heart leading you to start a conversation with a stranger or to make a phone call to someone you haven't spoken to in a while? What was the outcome?

6. Micah 6:8 offers us great advice on how to live in a way that exemplifies Jesus:

> He has told you, O man, what is good;
> And what does the LORD require of you
> But to do justice, to love kindness,
> And to walk humbly with your God?

Doing justice simply means to treat others in a righteous and just way that honors and glorifies God.

To love kindness (some translations say "loyalty" or "mercy") is to love others the same way He loves us. Finally, to walk humbly before God means to be obedient to His will. In what ways can you be just, love kindness/mercy, and walk humbly with God?

7. In 1 Corinthians 9:24 Paul writes,

> Do you not know that those who run in a race all run, but only one receives the prize? Run in such a way that you may win.

What does this verse mean to you as you live with an eternal perspective in mind?

8. While I don't know the full picture of what heaven will be like, I imagine God showing us the things we have done that have made a difference in the lives of others. Like inviting a friend to church, praying for someone, showing kindness when no one else would. How has someone made an eternal impact on your life?

9. How can you do the same for someone else?

10. What can you do right now to begin (or continue) to live a life of significance and leave a legacy for Jesus?

## WRAP UP

Today we have learned that what really matters is loving God and loving others. And through this life stance, we can make a difference in the lives of others and leave an eternal impact. Let's close our time together in prayer. Here are some ideas from this session that can guide our conversation with God:

- Thank God for giving you His Son, Jesus, so that you may live an abundant life to bless, to serve, and to make a difference in the lives of others.
- Ask God to show you opportunities where you can take a stand for others and make a difference.
- Pray for wisdom in how you spend your time, your resources, and your talents in ways that honor God and leave a lasting impact on others.
- Thank God that He has a plan and a purpose for your life, and continually pray that He unfolds that unique blueprint. Ask Him for strength to fight on the front lines for Jesus and bring others into His kingdom.

## INDIVIDUAL REFLECTION, STUDY, AND ACTION

1. It might have been Thomas Jefferson who said, "One man with courage is a majority." Taking a stand for someone or something is not the easiest thing to do. If it were, everyone would be doing it. But when we're willing to do this, incredible things can happen.

   Think about your life and those in it, particularly the ones you see every day but may not pay much attention to. Like the homeless person you pass on your way to work, or the kid in class who gets made fun of, or the man or woman who just got diagnosed with an illness. How can you stand up for one person in your life, whether praying for or serving them in some way?

2. Think about the world around you. Is there a particular cause or organization that touches your heart? Perhaps

you feel compassion toward battered women, orphans, or people diagnosed with a particular debilitating or terminal illness. How can you take a stand for that cause?

3. We often spend so much time and energy worrying and thinking about things that don't really matter, like what car we want to drive, what we want to do on our birthday, how many loads of laundry we have to do each day, whether or not that person likes us, where we are going on our family vacation.

   Today, spend time reflecting on what your life means, what it's about, what it stands for. If you are not satisfied with how you are spending your time, your energy, or your resources, write down how you would like your life to matter. Whether you are a parent, a student, an athlete, a teacher, have a great job or are looking for one, graduated from business school with an MBA or barely passed high school, write down the legacy you want to leave. What do you want to accomplish? What do you want others to say about you? What lasting impressions do you want to remain behind after you die?

MY PRAYER FOR YOU

*Dear Jesus, give the person reading this book the courage to do something that impacts eternity, in word or in deed, and the wisdom and the ability to do it well. May their obedience to You and their actions leave a legacy bigger than themselves, bigger than their platform. Help them to keep choosing over and over and over again to make a difference. Honor their commitment to serve You and to live a life that serves others. Amen.*

"Many people don't even try to reach out and help others because they're scared their efforts won't matter or won't make much of a difference. Have courage and at least try. Even if you fail, at least you will have planted a seed. You don't know what God can do with one step forward, with a raised hand, with a heart that says yes, with five loaves and two fish, with a slingshot and a few stones. Don't limit what He can do based on how you limit yourself. Be yourself, and let God be God."

—from *Shaken*

# About the Author

Tim Tebow is a two-time national champion, Heisman trophy winner, and first-round NFL draft pick. After playing in the NFL for the Denver Broncos and the New York Jets, Tebow joined the SEC Network. In addition to his role on *SEC Nation,* the network's traveling road show, Tebow also contributes to a variety of other ESPN platforms. Through everything, Tim's true passion remains the work of the Tim Tebow Foundation, which he began in 2010. The foundation's mission is to bring faith, hope, and love to those needing a brighter day in their darkest hour of need. The foundation is fulfilling that mission every day by serving thousands of deserving children around the world.

# TIM TEBOW FOUNDATION™

FAITH • HOPE • LOVE

---

To continue to fight for those who can't fight for themselves, a portion of proceeds from each book sold will be donated to the **Tim Tebow Foundation** to help further their mission of:

***Bringing Faith, Hope and Love to those needing a brighter day in their darkest hour of need.***

**The foundation is currently fulfilling this mission every day by...**

- Providing life-changing surgeries through the **Tebow CURE Hospital** to children of the Philippines who could not otherwise afford care.
- Creating a worldwide movement through **Night to Shine**, an unforgettable prom experience, centered on God's love, for people with special needs.
- Building **Timmy's Playrooms** in children's hospitals around the world.
- Fulfilling the dreams of children with life-threatening illnesses through the **W15H** program.
- Encouraging volunteer service to others through **Team Tebow** and **Team Tebow Kids**.
- Supporting housing, meals, medical treatment and education for orphans around the world though our **Orphan Care** program.
- Providing **Adoption Aid** financial assistance to families who are making the courageous choice to adopt a child with special needs internationally.

**...simply put, Serving Children and Sharing God's Love!**

To learn more about these initiatives and the continued growth of the foundation's outreach ministries, visit **www.timtebowfoundation.org.**